MINECRAFT ZONE

« MINECRAFT »
CONSTRUCTION

UNOFFICIAL GAMER GUIDE

Zelda Wagner

Lerner Publications ◆ Minneapolis

Lerner Publications Company
An imprint of Lerner Publishing Group, Inc.
241 First Avenue North
Minneapolis, MN 55401 USA

For reading levels and more information, look up this title at www.lernerbooks.com.

Main body text set in ITC Franklin Gothic Std.
Typeface provided by Adobe Systems.

Editor: Cole Nelson **Designer:** Mary Ross **Photo Editor:** Angel Kidd
Lerner team: Martha Kranes

Library of Congress Cataloging-in-Publication Data

Names: Wagner, Zelda, 2000– author.
Title: Minecraft construction : unofficial gamer guide / Zelda Wagner.
Description: Minneapolis : Lerner Publications, [2025] | Series: Minecraft zone (UpDog Books) | Includes bibliographical references and index. | Audience: Ages 8–11 | Audience: Grades 2–3 | Summary: "There's no end to what you can make in the world of Minecraft. Whether they want to build a small shelter or a big city, readers will love exploring Minecraft building tools and materials"— Provided by publisher.
Identifiers: LCCN 2023051250 (print) | LCCN 2023051251 (ebook) | ISBN 9798765626481 (lib. bdg.) | ISBN 9798765629024 (pbk.) | ISBN 9798765635407 (epub)
Subjects: LCSH: Buildings—Computer-aided design—Juvenile literature. | Minecraft (Game)—Juvenile literature.
Classification: LCC TH437 .W295 2025 (print) | LCC TH437 (ebook) | DDC 794.8/5—dc23/eng/20231107

LC record available at https://lccn.loc.gov/2023051250
LC ebook record available at https://lccn.loc.gov/2023051251

Manufactured in the United States of America
1-1009901-51982-9/22/2023

TABLE OF CONTENTS

MATERIALS

Minecraft is an open-world game.

That means players can choose how they play.

Players craft items using materials.

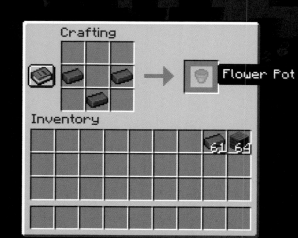

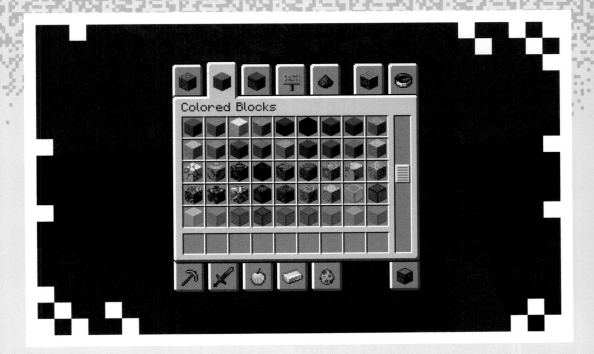

Some materials are shaped like blocks.
Others are shaped like different objects.

« UP NEXT! »

COLLECTING MATERIALS.

GATHERING AND MINING

In Survival Mode, players gather wood by chopping trees.

They dig dirt from the
ground with a shovel.

They place the dirt where they want it. Placing water by the dirt helps plants grow.

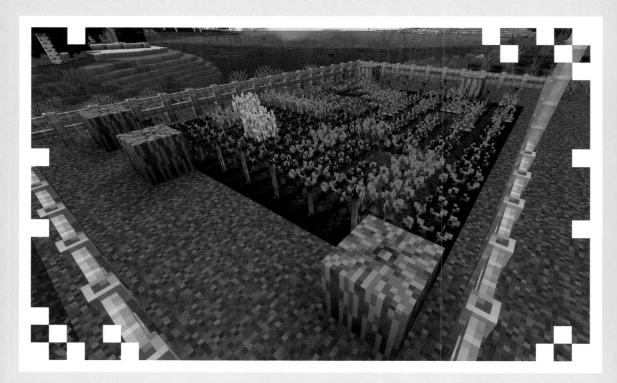

Planting flowers or wheat
can create a garden.

Some materials are
mined with a pickaxe.

Players mine for ores to make better tools. Coal is mined to make torches.

Players use materials by
putting them in the hotbar.

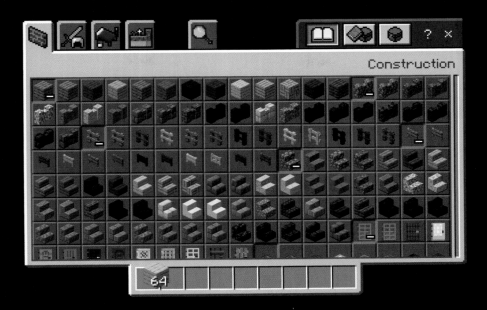

There are lots of
materials to build with.

« GaMe »
BREaK!

Here are ten simple tools to help you build:

1. Pickaxe

2. Axe

3. Shovel

4. Crafting table

5. Furnace

6. Stonecutter

UP NEXT!

UNLIMITED IDEAS.

CREATING FROM SCRATCH

Shelters help players stay safe in Survival Mode.

Cube shelters are
easy to build.

In Creative Mode, players can use unlimited materials.

Redstone can power
lights and machines.

Players can make
castles or fortresses.

Or they can build
a space needle!

Players can even make cool vehicles or landmarks from real life.

« UP NEXT! »

BUILDING CITIES.

BIG CITY BUILDS

Building a city is fun.

Players look at photos and maps for guidance. They build things to scale.

That means objects in the city
look realistic next to one another.

For example, skyscrapers
are built taller than trees.

You can build anything in *Minecraft*!

Glossary

Creative Mode: a gameplay setting where players have all resources available and do not need to worry about survival

landmark: an important building, monument, or place

scale: the size of something compared to something else

shelter: something that covers or protects

Survival Mode: a gameplay setting where players gather materials and build while defending against dangers

Check It Out!

CodaKid: 13 *Minecraft* Builds You Didn't Know You Could Make (No Mods)
https://codakid.com/minecraft-builds/

Kiddle: *Minecraft* Facts for Kids
https://kids.kiddle.co/Minecraft

Miller, Marie-Therese. *34 Amazing Facts about* Minecraft. Minneapolis: Lerner Publications, 2024.

Minecraft Official Site
https://minecraft.net/en-us

Morison, S. D. *Your Unofficial Guide to Building Cool* Minecraft *Railroads*. New York: Enslow, 2023.

Wagner, Zelda. Minecraft *Creative Mode: Unofficial Gamer Guide*. Minneapolis: Lerner Publications, 2025.

Index

Photo Acknowledgments

Image credits: Various screenshots by Angel Kidd, Heather Schwartz, Julia Zajac, and Linda Zajac. Other images: screenshot from Google Street View, p. 26. Design elements: Anatolii Poliashenko/Getty Images; filo/Getty Images.